Everybody Electric Bass Method 1

A Step-by-Step Approach

Michael Trowbridge
Philip Groeber

MW00582161

able

CONTENTS

Production: Frank J. Hackinson
Production Coordinator: Philip Groeber
Cover Design: Andi Whitmer
Engraving: Tempo Music Press, Inc.
Printer: Tempo Music Press, Inc.

Audio Tracks: Michael Trowbridge, John T. Kirkhum
Video: Michael Trowbridge; C. D. Hylton High School,
Woodbridge, VA Television Productions - Ashley Ellison,
Kiaya Jeusi, Brooklynn Chatman, Mya Kenton,
Mirachelle Canada, Director

THE FJH MUSIC COMPANY INC.
Frank J. Hackinson

ISBN-13: 978-1-61928-228-5

PARTS OF THE ELECTRIC BASS

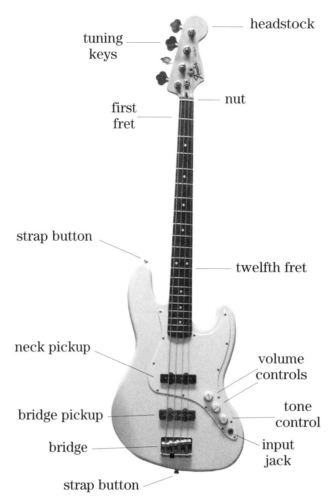

headstock

tuning keys

nut

first fret

strap button

twelfth fret

neck pickup

volume controls

tone control

bridge pickup

bridge

input jack

strap button

The solid-body electric bass can be used for a wide range of musical styles. Finger-style technique is usually best, but using a pick may be an option. Always practice with an amplifier.

THE BASS AMP

A one-piece combo-type amp is a good choice for your first amp. Turn on the amp and adjust the tone controls to a "flat" setting, which means the treble, mid, and bass knobs are at 12 o'clock. Then you can adjust as needed.

Cable Tips:

1) Place the cable through the handle on the top of the amp before inserting the end in the amp's input jack.

2) Loop the cable through your strap by the strap button near the bridge. This is a simple solution to prevent embarrassing moments when you accidentally step on your cable and the plug is pulled out of the input jack.

3) Plug the cable into your bass and your amp *before* you turn the amp on.

4) When you are finished playing, turn the amp off first, then remove the cable. Unplug the amp and keep it in a safe place.

HOLDING THE ELECTRIC BASS

Sitting

The bass should rest comfortably on your lap. The right leg may be crossed over the left leg for added support.

Standing

A strap is used to hold the bass in correct playing position. The strap may also be used in the sitting position. Loop your cable between the strap and body of the bass so it will not pull out if the cable is accidentally stepped on.

The Left Hand

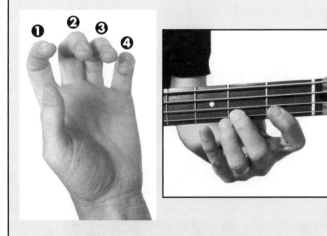

- The left-hand fingers are numbered 1, 2, 3, 4 as shown.
- Press with the fingertip directly *behind* the fret. Use just enough pressure to produce a clear sound. For best results, the left-hand fingernails should be kept short.
- The thumb should touch lightly on the back of the neck of the bass opposite the second finger. It remains in a natural position. The palm does not touch the back of the neck.

The Right Hand

- The index (i) and middle (m) fingers are used to sound the strings of the bass. A pick may be used to achieve a brighter sound.
- Start by resting your thumb on a pickup.
- Let your fingers hang comfortably over the strings.
- Using the pads of your fingers, alternate $i \ m \ i \ m$ as you play.

MUSIC FUNDAMENTALS

THE STAFF

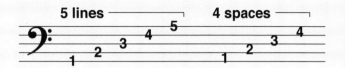

Music is written on the **staff**, which has five lines and four spaces.

THE BASS CLEF

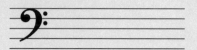

The **bass** (or **F**) **clef** is placed at the beginning (left side) of each staff of bass music.

LINE NOTES

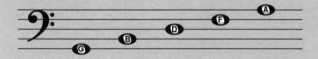

Each **line** has a letter name:

Good **B**assists **D**o **F**ine **A**lways

SPACE NOTES

Each **space** has a letter name:

All **C**ows **E**at **G**rass

PITCH

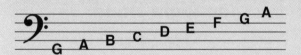

Pitch is the highness or lowness of a music tone. The higher the pitch, the higher a note is placed on the staff. The lower the pitch, the lower a note is placed on the staff. The names of notes come from the music alphabet A–G.

NOTE VALUES

o	**whole note**	= 4 beats
𝅗𝅥.	**dotted half note**	= 3 beats
𝅗𝅥	**half note**	= 2 beats
♩	**quarter note**	= 1 beat
♪	**eighth note**	= ½ beat

Note values (o 𝅗𝅥. 𝅗𝅥 ♩ ♪) indicate the duration (**rhythm**) of each pitch. Each musical note indicates the pitch to be played *and* how long to let the tone sound.

BAR LINES AND MEASURES

bar line   ending bar line

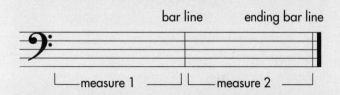

measure 1   measure 2

Bar lines divide the staff into equal parts called **measures**. An **ending bar line** is used to show the end of a piece of music.

THE TIME SIGNATURE

The $\frac{4}{4}$ (four-four) **time signature** tells us:

$\mathbf{4}$ = four beats per measure

$\mathbf{4}$ = the quarter note (♩) gets one beat

Count: 1   2   3   4

TUNING THE BASS

It is very important that your bass be tuned correctly each time you practice.

1. Electronic tuner

The *easiest* way to tune your bass is with an **electronic tuner**, which comes with simple instructions. Smart phone apps and electronic tuners are inexpensive and are used by many professional bassists as well as beginning students. Tuners that clip onto the headstock as shown above make tuning the bass easier, and are very accurate.

2. Piano keyboard

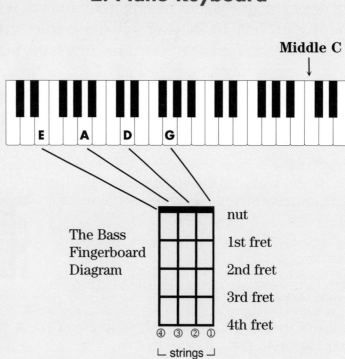

The Bass Fingerboard Diagram

Your bass can be tuned to a **piano**, an **organ**, or an **electronic keyboard**. Important: Notice the location of Middle C on the chart above.

*Video 1

* Visit www.fjhmusic.com/G1062 to view all 10 videos!

3. Tuning the bass to itself (relative tuning)

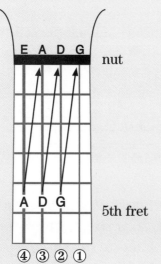

Assuming that string ④ is correctly tuned to E:			
PRESS	**STRING**	**TO GET THE PITCH**	**TO TUNE OPEN STRING**
the 5th fret of	④	**A**	③
the 5th fret of	③	**D**	②
the 5th fret of	②	**G**	①

TRACK
2 Tuning notes: G D A E

TABLATURE

Tablature is a notation system that has been around for several hundred years. The use of tablature became more prominent in the 1980s due to popular music becoming increasingly more technical, especially in the rock world.

Tablature does not give you as much information as the five-line staff (standard notation), but becomes a big help by showing you the correct string and fret for any given note. So, tablature helps in finding the location of a note, but does not usually give you: note values, the name of the note, dynamics, articulations, or fingering.

How to Use Tablature (TAB)

The four horizontal lines represent each of the four strings on a bass.
The first (thinnest) string (G) is the top line.

The fourth (thickest) string is (E) the bottom line.

The numbers in the TAB staff tell you the correct fret to play on a string.

0	=	open string (no fingers)	1 = 1st fret		2 = 2nd fret
3	=	3rd fret	4 = 4th fret		

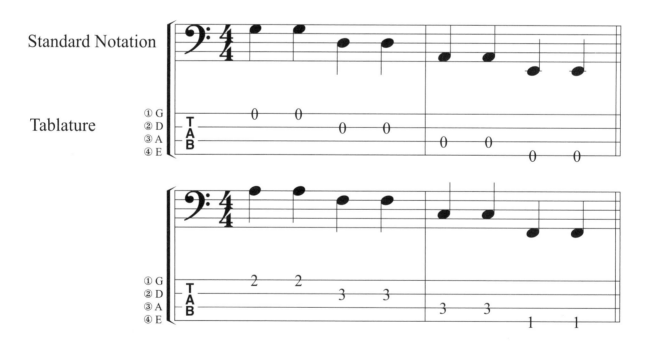

As you begin your new journey to becoming an excellent bass player, be sure to take the task of learning to read music notation seriously. You can see that tablature can be a handy tool, enabling you to find the location of the notes on the bass fingerboard easily. Tablature, tied together with improving your skills in reading music notation will thoroughly prepare you for a successful future as a musician.

With this in mind, use the Free Download information on the inside back cover to access several resources that will prove to be very helpful in sharpening your music notation and tablature reading skills.

G1062

RIGHT-HAND TECHNIQUE

Resting your thumb on the pickup will give your hand more stability. As your technique progresses you may want to play without this support. Your index (*i*) and middle (*m*) fingers will be alternating as you play. Repeat the mantra: Play that bass, *alternate*!

If you are looking for a brighter sound, move your right hand closer to the bridge.
For a fatter sound (similar to an upright bass) move your right hand toward the neck.
Your thumb can also be used to vary the sound. Experimenting with sound is important!

Rest Stroke *Use the rest stroke technique to bring out the true sound of the electric bass. After a finger plays a string, the finger playing the note "falls" off and comes to "rest" on the string below it. For example, when the index finger plays a note on the G string it will come to "rest" on the D string. Practice using the rest stroke while playing the TAB below. (HINT: See the Tech Tip box on page 11.)*

index finger *playing* the 1st string

index finger *resting* on the 2nd string

3 First String Open, G

	i	*m*	*i*	*m*	*i*	*m*	*i*	*m*

Count: 1   2   3   4   1   2   3   4

Second String Open, D

	i	*m*	*i*	*m*	*i*	*m*	*i*	*m*

Count: 1   2   3   4   1   2   3   4

Third String Open, A

	i	*m*	*i*	*m*	*i*	*m*	*i*	*m*

Count: 1   2   3   4   1   2   3   4

Fourth String Open, E

	i	*m*	*i*	*m*	*i*	*m*	*i*	*m*

Count: 1   2   3   4   1   2   3   4

REST STROKE UPDATE

You cannot technically use a rest stroke when playing a note on the fourth string E, because your right-hand finger cannot come to rest on a string that is not there. But by using the same motion as you used on the other strings you can still achieve that great rest stroke sound!

The left hand is responsible for fingering the correct notes. Whenever a finger is placed on a fret the length of the string is shortened, creating a higher-pitched note.

Keep your hand relaxed. Avoid any unnecessary stretching that might cause a strain.

Keep your hand curved around the neck of the bass as shown. Keep your thumb behind the center of the neck and opposite of the 2nd finger. Play with the pads of your fingers.

Place your fingertips directly behind the fret, not on top of it. Carefully listen to each note you play to be sure that you are pleased with the way that it sounds. You need to develop the ability to create a clear sound without any buzzing noises.

Video 2

Common Left-Hand Finger Positions for the Bass

One of the most important decisions you will be making as a bassist is choosing the best left-hand fingering for the music you are playing. When looking at the frets on your bass as you are playing you will see that the lower frets are very wide, and as you go higher on the neck the frets gradually get smaller. Your fingerings must be flexible as you move around on the bass.

Play each example several times on every string, remembering to alternate the *i, m* fingers.

First Position, 1-2-4

This is the position used in the beginning of this book, using the open strings. This position is used on the lower frets where the frets are farther apart. Fingers 1, 2, and 4 are spread over the first three frets. The 3rd finger is not used as often as the other fingers on the first five frets.

First Position   *Play two times.*

open string	2nd finger	4th finger	4th finger	4th finger	2nd finger	open string	open string
i	*m*	*i*	*m*	*i*	*m*	*i*	*m*
0	2	3	3	3	2	0	0

④

T
A
B

The 1-2-4 Movable Position

This position is similar to the **First Position** but will not be using very many open strings. This hand position can be moved around to different frets or **positions**.
The fret where the first finger is located indicates the name of the L.H. (left hand) position.

First Position

1st finger	2nd finger	4th finger	4th finger	4th finger	2nd finger	1st finger	1st finger
i	*m*	*i*	*m*	*i*	*m*	*i*	*m*
1	2	3	3	3	2	1	1

Play two times.

Second Position

1st finger	2nd finger	4th finger	4th finger	4th finger	2nd finger	1st finger	1st finger
i	*m*	*i*	*m*	*i*	*m*	*i*	*m*
2	3	4	4	4	3	2	2

Play two times.

Third Position

1st finger	2nd finger	4th finger	4th finger	4th finger	2nd finger	1st finger	1st finger
i	*m*	*i*	*m*	*i*	*m*	*i*	*m*
3	4	5	5	5	4	3	3

Play two times.

The 1-2-3-4 Movable Position

This position is mostly used on the higher frets where the frets are closer together. In this position, fingers 1, 2, 3, and 4 spread over four frets, one finger for each fret.
On ascending notes, leave the finger on the string until all fingers are down. Holding all fingers down will help the 4th finger which is the weakest finger.

Fifth Position

1st finger	2nd finger	3rd finger	4th finger	4th finger	3rd finger	2nd finger	1st finger
i	*m*	*i*	*m*	*i*	*m*	*i*	*m*
5	6	7	8	8	7	6	5

Play two times.

FRET MARKERS
Use the fret markers on the edge of the neck of the bass to help you find the higher fret numbers quickly. Most basses use a dot to indicate frets 3, 5, 7, and 9. The 12th fret has two dots. Go ahead and find them now!

The 12th fret is an important fret, the notes on the 12th fret are one **octave** higher than the open string. For example, the 1st string open is a G, the note on the 12th fret of the 1st string is also a G, but it is one **octave** higher. Octaves are notes that are 8 letter names apart (see the *Discovery* box page 14 and the *Octave Box* on page 31).

NOTES ON THE FIRST STRING

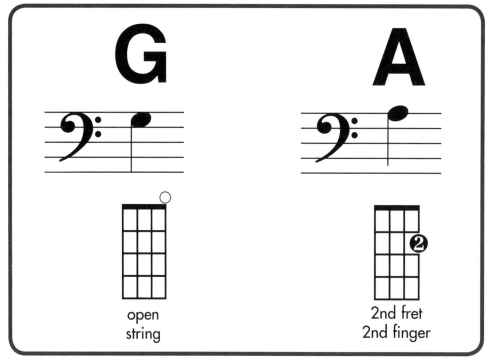

G — open string

A — 2nd fret, 2nd finger

QUARTER NOTES

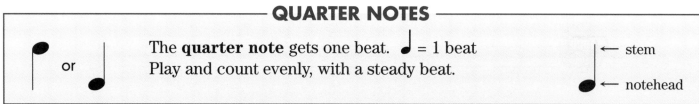

The **quarter note** gets one beat. ♩ = 1 beat
Play and count evenly, with a steady beat.

← stem

← notehead

Numbers next to the noteheads (0, 1, 2, 3, 4) indicate left-hand fingering.
i (index finger) and *m* (middle finger) indicate the alternation pattern for the right hand.

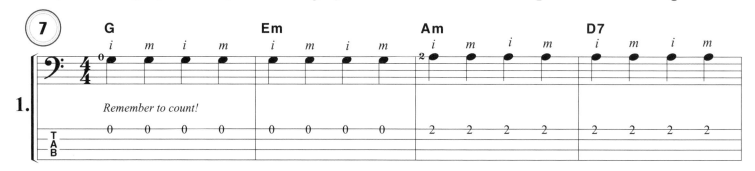

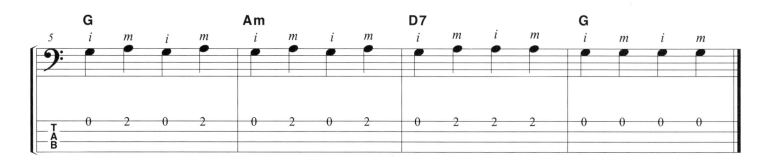

*Chord names (G, Em, Am, D7, etc.) are placed over the music and indicate the **harmony**. A guitar or piano player will be able to play along with you using the chord names. In this book you will also learn what bassists can play by only using the chord names.*

HALF NOTES

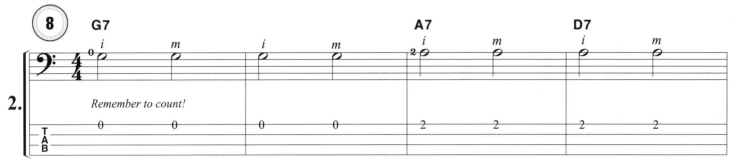

The **half note** gets two beats. $\mathbf{\downarrow}$ = 2 beats
Be sure to let the half note ring for two full beats.

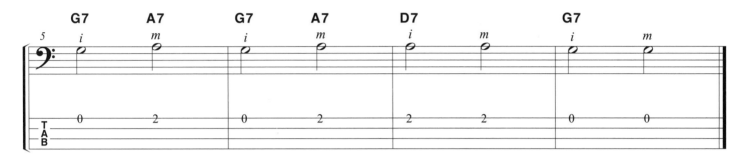

Remember to use the rest stroke (page 7) to get a good tone.
Listen carefully as you play, or even better, record yourself.
Work on your technique to acquire a firm, pleasant tone,
not so loud that the tone sounds distorted.

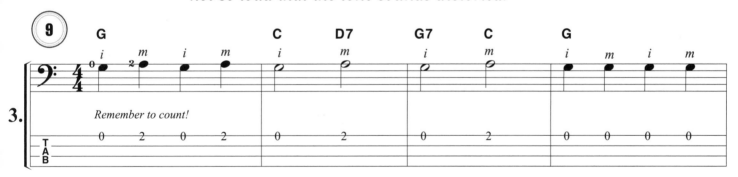

WHAT'S UP (or DOWN)?

Common sense would dictate that when you are playing bass, the string closest to the floor would be the lowest string...but just the opposite is true! The string closest to the floor is actually the highest string because it is the highest in **pitch**! Look at it is like this, the thicker the string, the lower the pitch!

Your left-hand controls pitch on the fingerboard. As you play any fret on the bass you shorten the length of the string, making the pitch higher.

NOTES ON THE SECOND STRING

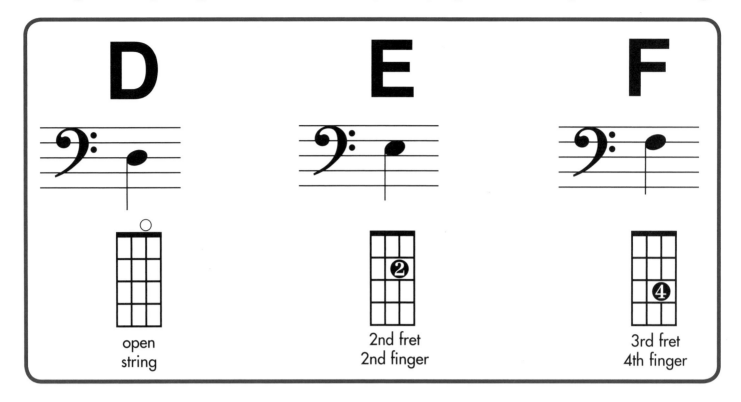

D — open string

E — 2nd fret / 2nd finger

F — 3rd fret / 4th finger

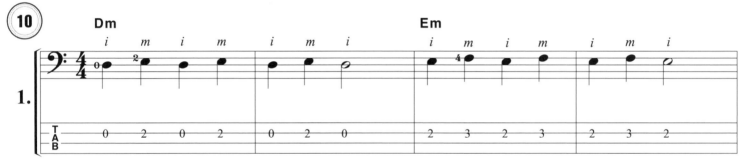

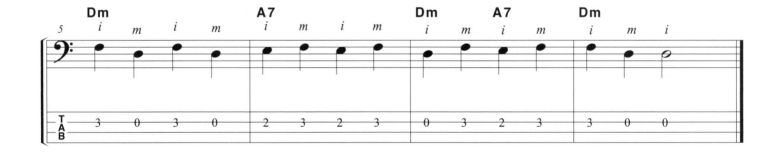

*The rake technique is a right-hand finger using a rest stroke,
and then using the same finger to play a note on the next lowest string.
See the example below.*

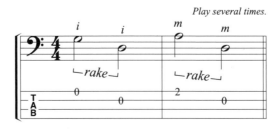

G106

PICK-UP NOTES

count: (1 2 3) 4

Pick-up notes are notes that come before the first complete measure. The combined value of the notes in the pick-up measure and the last measure are equal to the number of beats indicated in the time signature.

11

2.

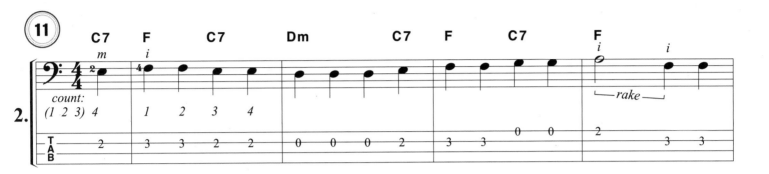

5

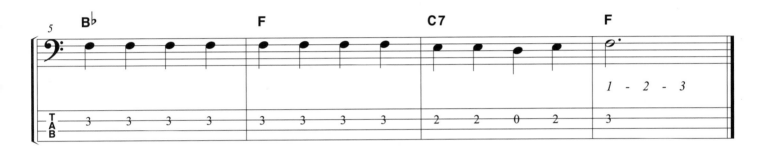

TIES

Count: (1 2 3 - 4 - 1 2 3 - 4

A **tie** connects two notes that are on the same line or space. Play the *first note only*, allowing it to sound for the combined value of both notes.

12

3.

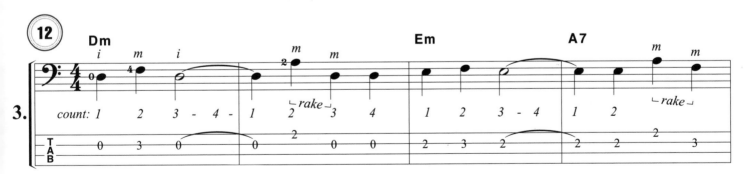

5

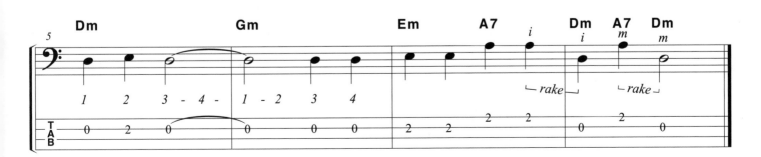

NOTES ON THE THIRD STRING

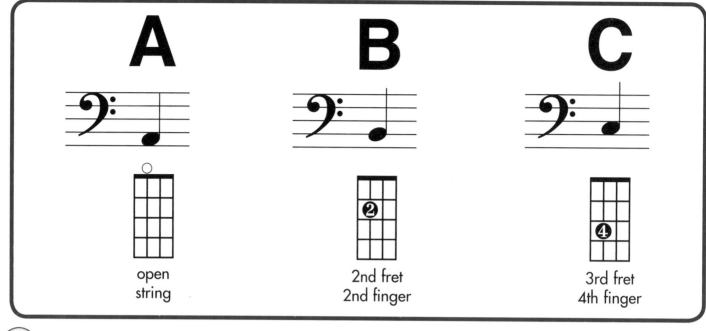

A — open string

B — 2nd fret, 2nd finger

C — 3rd fret, 4th finger

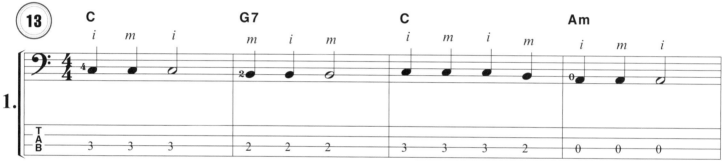

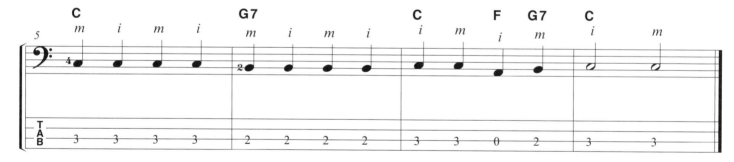

The **Discovery** icons are opportunities to use your new-found bass knowledge. You will learn to play interesting **riffs** (short musical ideas), and other ideas that will spark your own creativity. There may be notes or techniques that you have not learned yet, but by looking at the TAB and watching the video you will be amazed at what you can do! Let's get started.

Below is a fun-to-play riff using **octaves** (notes that are 8 steps apart). Use the fret markings (page 9) to find the 12th fret quickly. Experiment by playing this pattern on the other three strings. The **repeat sign** means to play the music two times.

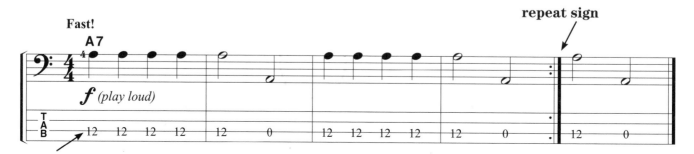

G1062

Music with a ¾ **time signature** gets three beats per measure. The quarter note still gets one count.

15

Am

 Remember to leave your fingers down on the string when playing ascending notes. This technique will improve the strength of the 4th finger.

DOTTED HALF NOTES

A dot placed after a note increases the value of the note by one half of its value. The **dotted half note** gets *three* beats.

$\mathrm{\circ}$ (2 beats) + $\mathrm{\downarrow}$ (1 beat) = $\mathrm{\circ.}$ (3 beats)

16

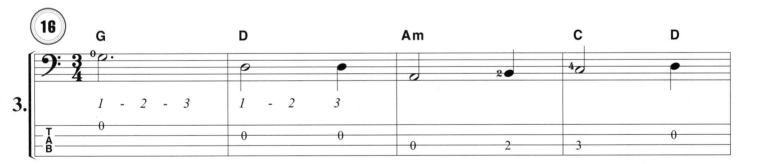

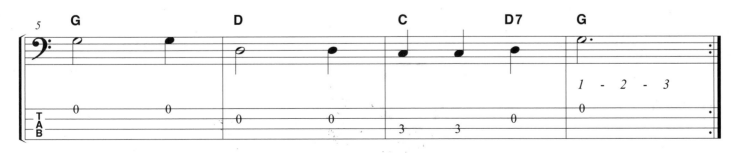

Did you remember to use the rake technique from page 12?

DYNAMICS

Dynamics are symbols and words that indicate how loud or soft to play. The following symbols are used in this book:

p = *piano* (soft)   *mf* = *mezzo forte* (medium loud)   *f* = *forte* (loud)

If the music has no dynamic level indicated, play *mf* (medium loud).

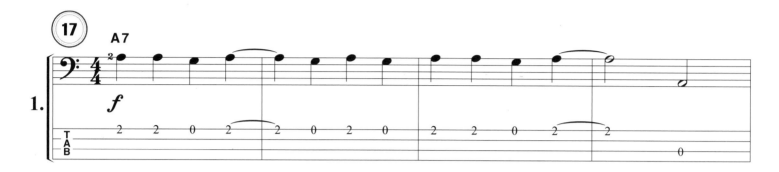

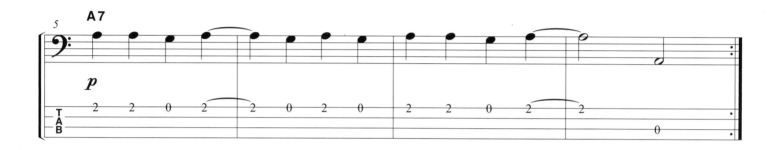

You will find that it is more difficult to play softer rather than louder. Softer does not mean slower, so keep a steady pulse. When there are two or more dynamic markings in a song, be sure you can hear the *contrast* between the dynamic levels!

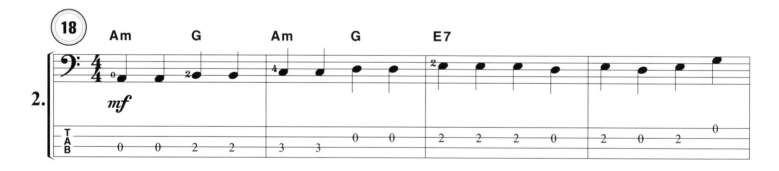

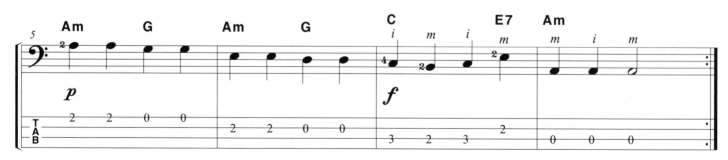

Dynamics are important, but not as important as playing the right notes at the right time, and getting a good sound. Dynamics are the "icing on the cake!"

G1062

WHOLE NOTES

O The whole note gets four beats. **O** = 4 beats
Four even counts must take place before you play the next note.
Count "**1-2-3-4**" for each whole note. **Always keep an even, steady beat.**
You should be able to hear the whole note sound for all four beats.

19

3.

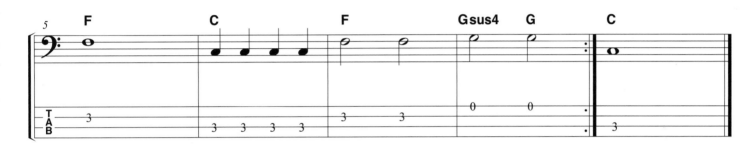

 When playing whole notes be sure that you are not rushing the beat (going too fast).

20

Whole notes cannot be used in 3/4 time.

4.

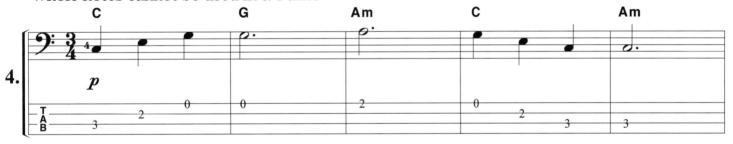

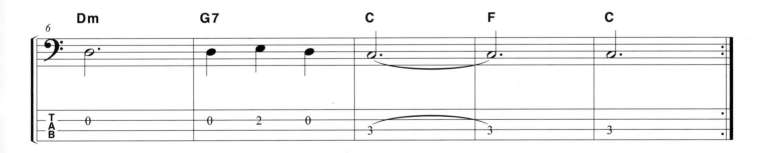

 *To be sure that you are playing with a steady beat, practice with a **metronome**. A metronome functions as a drummer, keeping you on a steady beat. This drummer does not have very many drums, but the tempo never varies once the song begins. The numbers on the metronome indicate how many beats there are in a minute (**bpm**). Metronomes are inexpensive and they are even available as free apps.*

NOTES ON THE FOURTH STRING

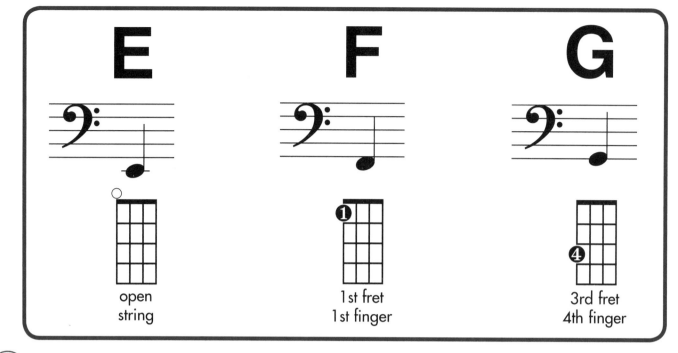

E — open string
F — 1st fret / 1st finger
G — 3rd fret / 4th finger

1.

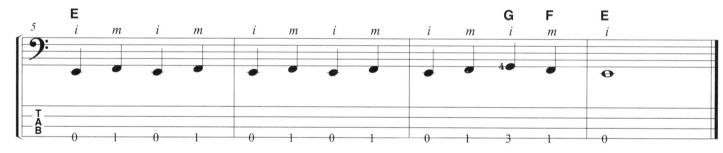

 Remember to always alternate your right-hand fingers!

The note A which is usually played as the open 3rd string is now played on the 5th fret of the 4th string. Most of the notes on the 3rd open-string A or higher can be played in two or more different places on the bass. Can you find more examples?

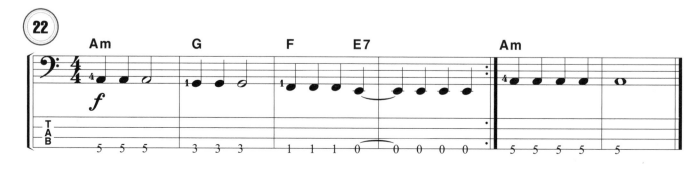

G1062

Here is a Chicago-Blues bass style that you will recognize from many rock and blues songs. There are no open strings, and your first finger starts on the 5th fret. Once you have the fingering pattern memorized, experiment by moving the pattern to different frets (positions).

YOUR SOUND IS IN YOUR FINGERS

Spend some time using the Chicago-Blues riff above (and other examples) to experiment with three different sounds that you can create with your right-hand fingers.
Place your right hand:

        1) near the end of the fingerboard to create a "round" sound.

        2) close to the bridge to create a short, detached sound.

        3) around the pickup area for a sound that works for most songs

You can make tone adjustments to your bass and amp, but 90% of your personal, identifying tone comes from your fingers. Listen!

You have learned all of the natural notes up to the 4th fret. Your note reading skills have greatly improved since you started this book! Now you can read music and are able to play correct notes at the correct time. Study the following Natural Note Chart very carefully.

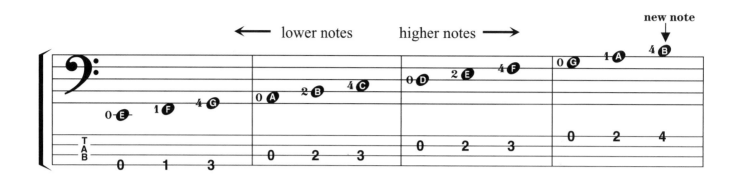

BASS BREAKDOWN
Things to Know!

Memorize the natural notes in First Position by playing them in ascending and descending (up-down) order, always observing correct right- and left-hand fingering. Use quarter notes with a strict, even tempo, gradually increasing in speed as your playing skills improve. *Practice this important exercise several times every day.*

There are three ways to use the natural note chart above.
  1) Read and study the music notation. Characteristics of the notation are:
     • the notes proceed in line-space-line-space order (step-wise motion)
     • the notes are in alphabetical order
  2) Read and study the tablature.
     • some of the TAB numbers skip; this is where the sharp (♯) and flat (♭) notes occur. Look ahead to pages 22 (sharps) and 28 (flats).
     • notice that the natural notes on the 2nd and 3rd strings share the identical pattern of open string, 2nd fret, 3rd fret
  3) Play the natural notes in First Position by ear only, reciting the names of the notes as you play.

The following short song uses all of the notes you have learned in First Position. Listen to the pattern of the notes in each measure. This would be a good exercise to memorize.

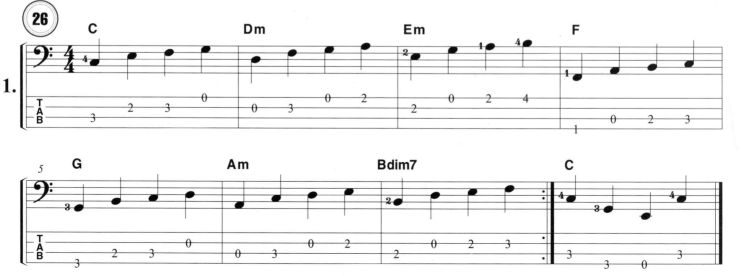

20

G1062

Chord Theory for Bassists, Part 1, Roots

A **chord** is playing three or more notes at the same time. Playing two notes at the same time is an **interval**. As a bassist you will not be playing chords like a guitar or piano player, but you will be playing the individual notes of the chords in your bass lines as well as intervals.

We will identify C as the **root** note *of any C-type chord* (C7, Cm, Cm7, etc.). D would be the **root** note *of any D-type chord* (D7, Dm, Dm7, etc.). As a bassist, you will be playing the roots of chords often. Look through the music in this book and discover how many times you are playing the root of the indicated chord names.

Imagine one day a member of your band hands you a piece of paper with the chords (no music, and barely readable) to a new song he wrote in 3/4 time that the band is going to learn. What can you do with these chord changes?

Am   C   D   F   Am   E7   Am   E7   Am

This is a very common situation that you will experience many times in your bass-playing career. Assume for now that the chords change at the beginning of each measure. The best way to start is to play the root of each chord, using dotted-half notes (3/4 time). In a band situation, since you will not have any music, you will need to find the correct roots by using your knowledge of the bass fingerboard. Find a solution on your own, then look at possible solutions below. No peeking!

Solution 1: Play roots only, moving to the *closest root* of the next chord.

Solution 2: Similar to Version 1 but uses different octaves. Any octave of the root note can be used.

Solution 3: Varies the octaves again but also adds more rhythm (♩) by connecting the roots with step-wise (A-B-C) movement whenever possible. For example, using the note B to connect the Am chord to the C chord.

Now try out these new tips for creating bass lines on songs that you already learned in this book. Concentrate on the chord names only, not the notes.

SHARPS

A **sharp** (♯) is a symbol that *raises* the pitch of a note by one fret (one half step).

For example, a G♯ on the 1st string will be played on the 1st fret.

An A♯ on the 1st string will be played on the 3rd fret.

A sharp stays in effect until the end of a measure.

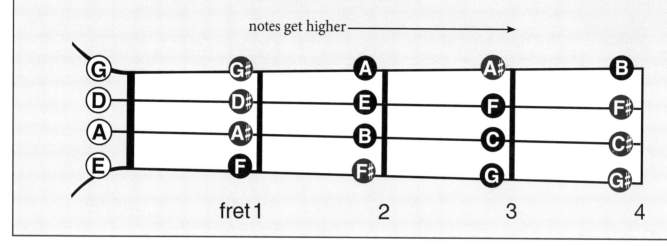

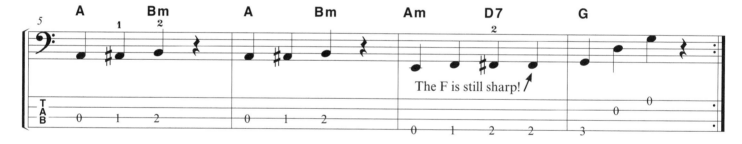

 Be sure to follow the left-hand fingering as indicated to greatly improve your technique! Your left-hand fingers can only easily cover four frets, so a certain amount of shifting (moving your hand up or down the fingerboard) will have to take place.

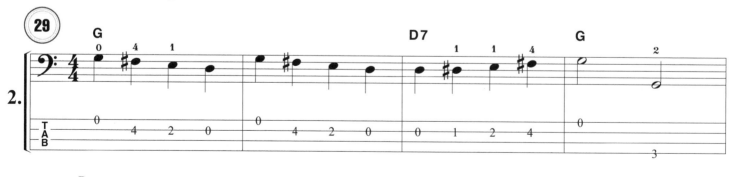

G1062

NATURALS

A **natural** (♮) *cancels* a sharp or flat (page 28) previously used.
For example, F♯ is played on the 2nd string, 4th fret.
F♮ is played on the 2nd string, 3rd fret.

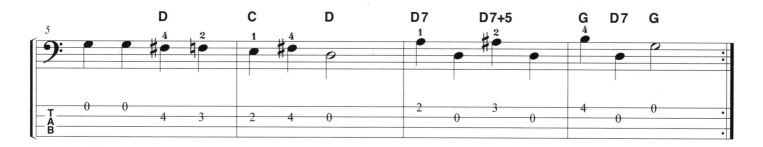

Power Play

Study 4 is easy to memorize and is an amazing finger warm-up exercise.
Set your metronome at 100 bpm and then gradually increase your speed,
keeping in mind that you must play smoothly and accurately at all times.
On ascending notes, leave your fingers on the string until all fingers are down.

Even though a sharp (or a flat) symbol is placed in the music "before" the notehead, we say G sharp, not sharp G. When we write the note name out as text, we write it as it is pronounced, G♯.

EIGHTH NOTES

A quarter note can be divided into two equal parts called **eighth notes**. A single eighth note has a **flag** (♪). Two or more eighth notes are usually connected by a **beam** (♫♫).

♪ = ½ beat   ♫ = 1 beat   ♫♫ = 2 beats

Counting Eighth Notes

The notes played on the beat (beats 1, 2, 3, 4) are called downbeats and are slightly accented. The notes counted as "and" (+) are the **upbeats**. As a bassist, one of your most important duties is to play a steady stream of eighth notes without any hesitation. Count as you play!

Consistently alternating your right-hand fingers with a rest stroke will help you keep a steady beat. Get out your metronome and set it to 60 bpm. Practice often with a metronome.

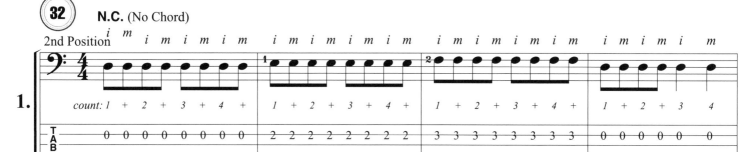

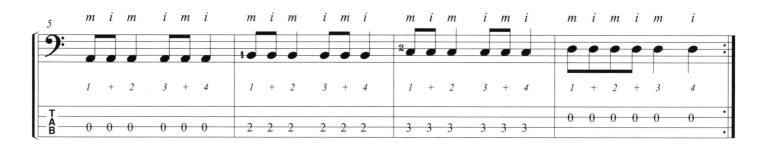

In No. 2 *shift* your left hand to 2nd Position. Keep your 1st finger on the 2nd fret and your 4th finger on the 4th fret. Carefully observe your right-hand technique.

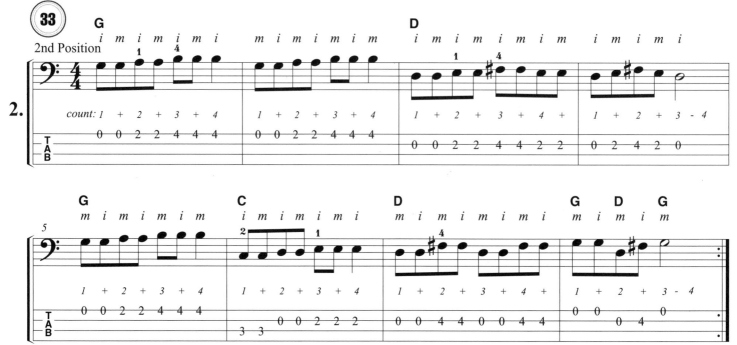

24

Super Session

Remember to use the rake technique when moving down to the next lowest-pitched string.

Bass Boogie

Let's play eighth notes on a Chicago-Blues bass style. This is a similar left-hand fingering pattern to the Discovery on page 19. The audio track demonstrates *two different styles* of playing eighth notes: straight eighths and swing eighths.

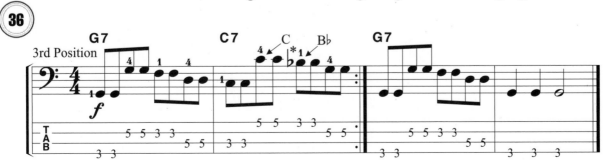

*Flats (♭) *lower* the pitch of a note by one fret.

PLAYING THE MELODY

Bassists need to know how to make a beautiful melody sing through their instrument. Beyond remembering how to play the right note at the right time, you need to concentrate on the music you are creating by listening. Use rest strokes with the other performance techniques you have learned so far to make beautiful music happen!

Molly Malone
Traditional Irish

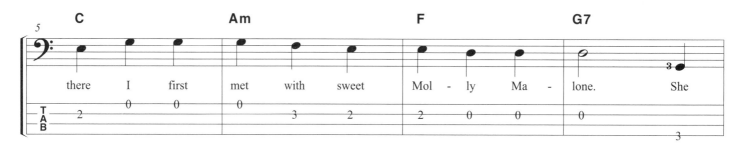

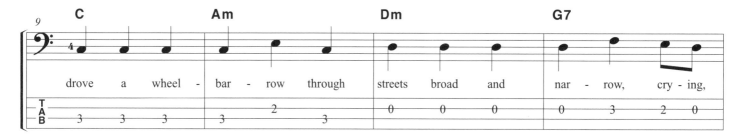

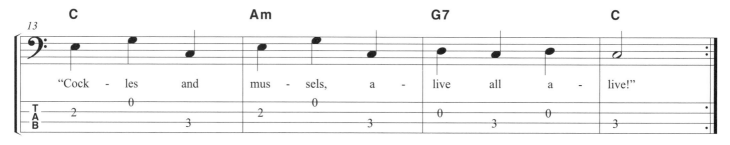

Developing Your Performance Technique

Learning to develop a beautiful tone takes more time than you may think. It is a lifetime mission, always listening carefully to what you play.

Here are two good ways to help you get started on this journey.
   1) *Memorize the music that you enjoy playing. This will allow you to listen more carefully by not concentrating so much on reading the music, fingering, counting, etc.*
   2) *Then you will be ready to record yourself performing. The first time you do this you will be amazed that the recording does not sound the way you envisioned it sounding. There are many free or inexpensive apps available to help you get started.*

G106

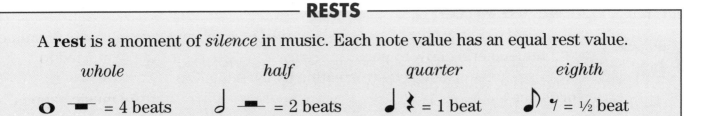

RESTS

A **rest** is a moment of *silence* in music. Each note value has an equal rest value.

whole	*half*	*quarter*	*eighth*
𝅝 ▬ = 4 beats	𝅗𝅥 ▬ = 2 beats	♩ 𝄽 = 1 beat	♪ 𝄾 = ½ beat

Moving Down

38

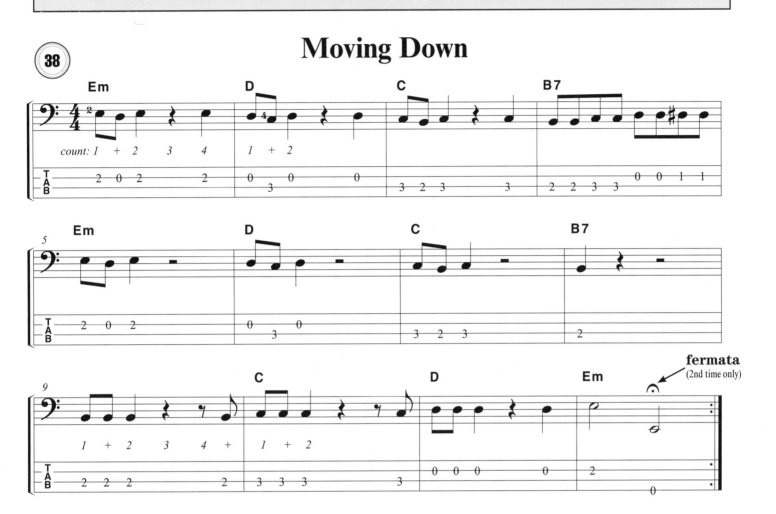

Dampen the strings when observing a rest. Releasing the pressure of a left-hand finger will stop a string from vibrating. To dampen an open string, use the fingers of the left or right hand to lightly touch the vibrating strings.

Another important bass style to know is the boogie pattern. By the end of this book be sure that you can play a boogie pattern and the Chicago-Blues riff (Discovery page 25) starting on any note.

39

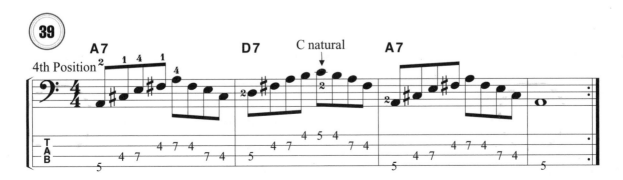

G1062

27

FLATS

A **flat** (♭) is a symbol that *lowers* the pitch of a note by one fret (one half step).

For example, a B♭ on the 1st string will be played on the 3rd fret.

An E♭ on the 2nd string will be played on the 1st fret.

A flat stays in effect until the end of a measure.

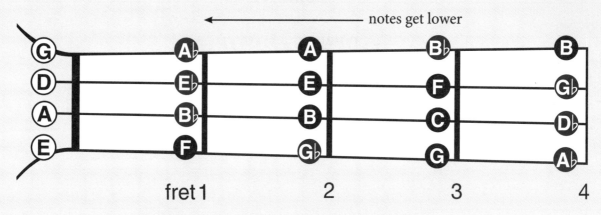

Sharps (♯), flats (♭), and naturals (♮) are known as **accidentals**.

DOTTED QUARTER NOTES

A dotted quarter notes receive 1½ beats. Dotted quarter notes are usually followed by an eighth note which receives only ½ beat. Together these two notes equal two beats.

♩. = 1½ beat   ♪ = ½ beat   ♩ = 2 beats

28

G106:

ENHARMONIC NOTES

Notes that have the same pitch but different names are called **enharmonic** notes. One of the notes will be a sharp note; the other will be a flat note, for example G♯ and A♭.

Both notes names are correct. Usually sharps are used in musical lines that are going up, while flats are used in musical lines going down. A good example is Study 4 below.

Below are five common sets of enharmonic notes. This principle applies to any octave of any note.

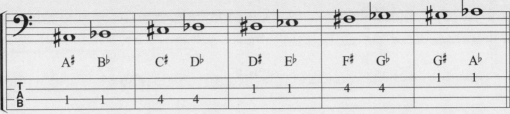

Open String Notes

The lowest possible note to play on any string is the open string. You need to move to the next lowest string on the 4th fret when an open string note is to be played as a flat.

 UNISONS

Another interesting fact to know about your bass is that the 5th fret note is the same pitch (**unison**) as the next highest-pitched open string. Go back and review page 5, No. 3, tuning the bass to itself, which is based on unisons.

In No. 3 below, you might notice that the natural sign in measures 2, 4, and 6 is not necessary. While this is true, many times you will see a natural directly after a bar line where the previous measure was using accidentals on the same note. This cautionary accidental is usually welcome because it lets the performer know with confidence what the correct note should be. When using Tablature, the natural is not really necessary.

 PLAYING IN POSITION

By using the indicated left-hand finger number and the tablature you should always be able to begin playing in the correct position.
For the rest of this book the starting position indications will only be included if the position is unclear.

Chord Theory for Bassists, Part 2, Roots and Fifths

We have identified the letter name of the chord as the **root** note of any chord type with that same letter name. The next most useful note to bass players is the 5th, that is the 5th note of the scale. Major scales will be introduced on page 32.

C is the root and the 1st note of the C scale. An easy way to find the fifth note of the C scale is to use your fingers as a visual aid. Hold your left hand in front of you, palm facing you.

Label your thumb as (1) C, index finger as (2) D, middle finger as (3) E, ring finger as (4) F, and little finger as (5) G. Use this easy to remember technique as a guide to finding the 5th.

Here are several possibilities how roots and 5ths fit into a bass-players world while playing in First Position.

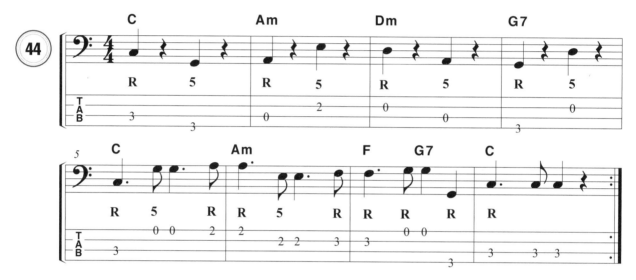

Here is a chart that shows roots and fifths of common chords.
Check to see that this chart is correct by counting on your fingers.

Fifth:	G	A	B	C	D	E
Root:	C	D	E	F	G	A

Moving into the upper positions with no open strings introduces two patterns that qualify as "need to know!"

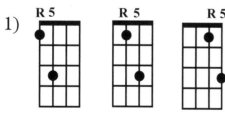

1)
a) 1st finger on root; 4th finger on 5th
b) root is lower than the 5th

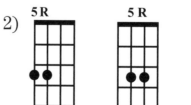

2)
a) use the same finger for each note, but any finger combination will work
b) root is higher than the 5th

Use both examples of these bass fingerboards to help you find and HEAR the roots and fifths. As long as you know what fret the root is on it is not difficult to see where the fifth is located. Play these six patterns using the rhythms for Track 44 above. Play as low and as high as you can reach on your bass.

THE OCTAVE

You have already learned a lot about octaves in this book:
- the 12th fret is one octave higher than the open string (page 9)
- you played a blues riff with octaves and learned octaves are eight notes apart (page 14)
- you played octaves in a bass line, Discovery (page 19)

Below are two important music examples showing you various patterns of octave locations throughout the bass fingerboard.

Using open strings.

No open strings. (Remember the phrase; Two strings over, Two frets higher!)

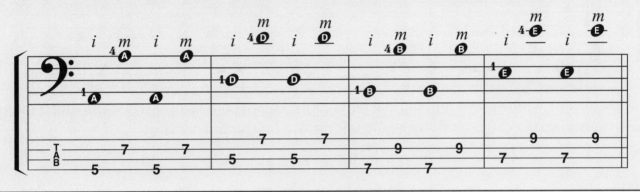

Play Nice

45

BE ADVENTUROUS!

Play and name every octave you can find, high and low, using the rhythm from *Play Nice*.

Use left-hand fingers 1 and 4 when there are no open strings!

Play that bass, alternate!

THE KEY OF C MAJOR

MAJOR SCALES

A **major scale** is a series of pitches arranged in ascending and descending order, beginning and ending with the same letter name. The distance between one letter name and the next is called a **step**. On the bass, a **whole step** is two notes, two frets apart; a **half step** is two notes, one fret apart. The pattern of whole (W) and half (H) steps for a major scale is as follows:

W   W   H   W   W   W   H

Memorize the C major scale, ascending and descending. Notice that the scale extends for eight notes (one octave), and begins and ends on C. Strive for a steady beat and evenness of tone. Learn even more about scales on page 46.

The C Major Scale, adding New Note C

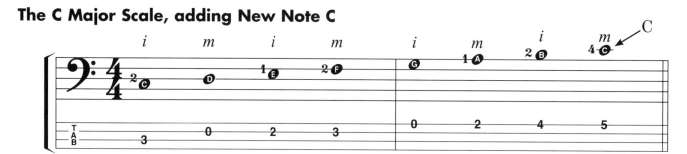

The pattern of whole steps and half steps is more easily understood when playing a major scale on one string only, such as the C major scale on the third string.

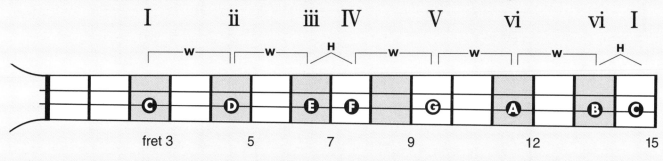

Songs using the notes of the C major scale are in the **Key of C**.
The first and last chords will probably be C. *The Can Can* is in the Key of C.

The Can Can
Jacques Offenbach

47 The three studies below use the notes of the C Major Scale.

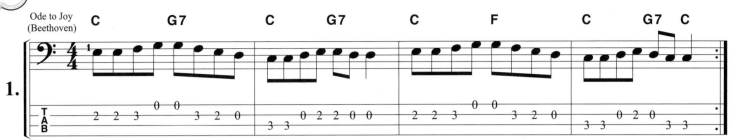

Ode to Joy
(Beethoven)

1.

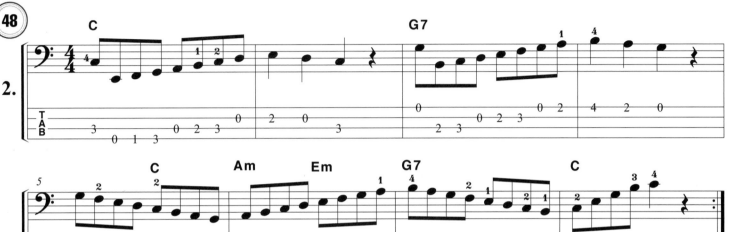

48

2.

49

3.

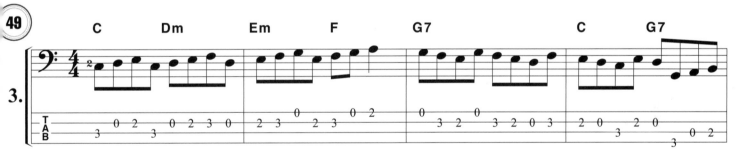

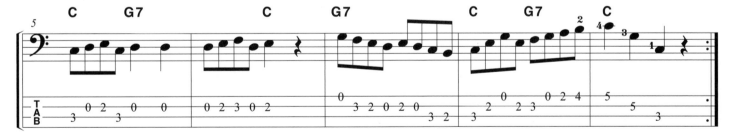

Eye-Training Tip When you observe notes proceeding in a line-space-line-space manner, you are looking at some type of a scale. Identifying scale patterns in the notation reminds you that you are playing music that is familiar to you. Many songs contain scale passages; look for them!

TWO HATS

You have acquired many music-reading skills since you began your bass study in this book, congratulations! Another responsibility of being a bass player is creating your own bass lines. In the following pages, you will learn how to play melody AND create a meaningful bass line!

Turn the page to learn more!

Chord Theory for Bassists, Part 3, Primary Chords

The study of the **Primary Chords** gives you a "big picture" look at chords that have been used the most often in almost every style of music for more than 600 years. Johann Sebastian Bach and Ludwig van Beethoven through The Beatles and Bruno Mars all used plenty of primary chords in their compositions. These chords have been used for all this time because "people like the way they sound!" There are technical reasons also, but basically we just like to hear them and play them. You can easily find these magical chords by using basic math, and counting on your fingers as before.

There are only three primary chords. When discussing them in the "big picture," each chord is assigned a Roman numeral I, IV, V (1, 4, 5). There are technical names used also: Tonic, Sub-Dominant, and Dominant. When used in a song these chords will be generally be identified by their letter name, but I, IV, and V are also widely used.

I (the KEY)	IV	V
Tonic	Sub-Dominant	Dominant

Using your fingers as a visual aid is an easy way to find the letter names of the Primary Chords. As before on page 30, hold your left hand in front of you, palm facing your head. Label your thumb as 1, index as 2, middle 3, ring 4, and pinky 5.

For example if a song is in the Key of C, think of your:

thumb as 1   (C) I Tonic (the key)
ring finger as 4   (F) IV Sub-Dominant
pinky finger as 5   (G) V Dominant

Here is a chart showing the primary chords in all 12 keys.

I (KEY)	C	G	D	A	E	B	F♯/G♭	D♭	A♭	E♭	B♭	F
IV	F	C	G	D	A	E	B/C♭	G♭	D♭	A♭	E♭	B♭
V	G	D	A	E	B	F♯	C♯/D♭	A♭	E♭	B♭	F	C

There is one more important fact to consider, why do some chord names have sharps or flats and other chord names do not?

The Roman numerals I, IV, and V pertain to each notes position in a Major Scale. The Key of C has no sharps or flats, but the other 11 scales all have a specific number of sharps or flats. For right now, you can see which Primary Chords use accidentals by looking at the bass fingerboards and the chord names as shown on page 35.

At this stage it would be a very good idea for you to learn to play all of the Major Scales in First Position, and then learn the same scales in movable positions. See page 46 for examples of these scales. Also, the **Everybody's Electric Bass: Scales and Arpeggios** publication (G1063) is recommended for this purpose. Studying the Bass Fingerboard Chart on the inside-back cover will also be helpful.

Music Master The Primary Chord theory that you just learned applies to all of the following chord types in any key: C, Cm, Cm7, C7, C9, Cdim7, C+5, etc. ALL use the same root note C. As a matter of fact, the guys in the band are counting on you to play the C! You are the foundation of the group and also the foundation of the key, in this case the key of C.

Below are six different keys using only the roots of the Primary Chords to play some music!

First Position

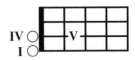

This is a movable pattern using open strings. You can also start this pattern on the open 3rd string A (key of A) or the open 2nd string D (key of D). The IV and the V chords are the interval of a 2nd (two frets) apart.

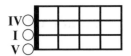

In this example the IV and V chords are separated by the interval of a 7th. The IV and the V chords sound much better when they are the interval of a 2nd, only two frets apart.

Higher Positions

These two examples start with the Tonic (I) on the 4th string but you can also start on the 3rd or 2nd strings. They are also movable, up and down the fingerboard to any fret that you can reach.

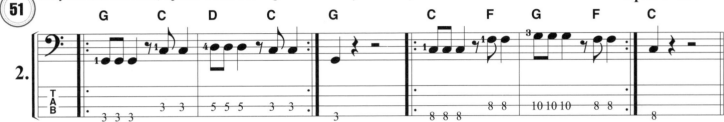

These two examples start with the Tonic (I) on the 3rd string but can also start on the 2nd and 1st strings. They are also movable, up and down the fingerboard to any fret that you can reach.

Here are several well-known rock tunes that use only the Primary Chords. Search for these songs on the internet and study them: La Bamba (Richie Valens), Louie Louie (The Kingsmen), Rock 'n' Roll (Led Zepplin), I Still Haven't Found What I'm Looking for (U2), and Hotel Yorba (The White Stripes).

At this time you need to develop a new skill, a musical process that you will enjoy doing the rest of your playing career, *playing by ear*.

A good song to start with is *La Bamba* by Richie Valens because it uses the primary chords in a repetitive order: I, IV, and then V. Listen to an audio recording and then by only using your ear, by trial and error identify what key (I) the song is in. Think of I as the home chord, songs usually begin and end at home. Once you know the key, find the IV and V chords, using the information above as a guide.

With a little perseverance you will be able to play bass along with this song (*without any written music*).

* The music in these examples is a popular rhythm pattern used in the 1963 hit, *Louie, Louie* by The Kingsmen.

Creating a Bass Line

Many popular songs sound great with the bass jumping from the root of one chord to the next. Nothing fancy, just good old rock and roll, similar to the examples on page 35. But, let's do more!

Two Ways to Musically Connect Chords in a Bass Line

1) Adding the 5th of the chord provides variety and generally creates a smooth transition to the next chord.
2) Use **passing tones** (step-wise motion) to connect the roots. This means using notes in line-space, line-space order, (alphabetical order). Also called a walking bass line, this technique uses a steady stream of quarter notes (or eighth notes) to create a bass line that seems to "walk". Jazz bassists pride themselves on their ability to create awesome walking bass lines.

Study the function of the notes in the following bass line.

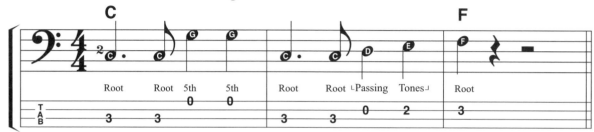

Identify every note below as a Root, a 5th, or a Passing Tone. Then play, striving to make a very smooth transition to each chord. Keep this in mind with every bass part you create!

G106

Using the whole step, half-step pattern on page 32, we will need to use an F♯ for the ... step and we need a whole step).

... e, **ascending and descending!**

The G Major ...

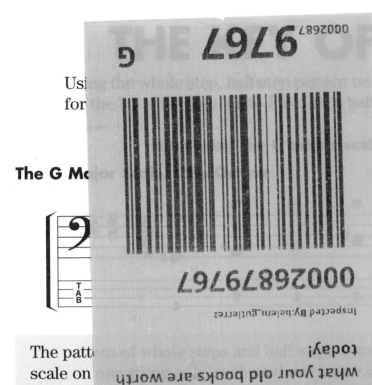

The pattern of whole steps and half ... re easily understood when playing a major scale on ... ale on the first string.

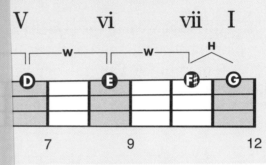

Songs using the notes of the G major scale are in the **Key of G**, identified by the sharp placed on the F line of every staff. This is called the **Key Signature**. The following version of *The Can Can* is in the Key of G. Compare the Key of G notes and chord names to *The Can Can* on page 32 in the Key of C.

(55)

The Can Can
Jacques Offenbach

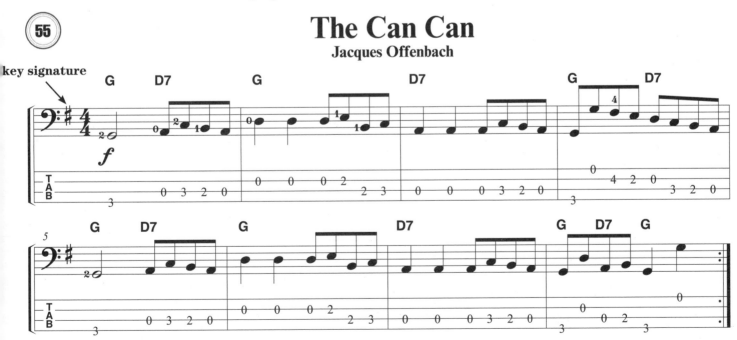

From this day forward, before you begin to play any new song be sure you identify what key the song is in by looking at the key signature! This is a common error that beginning musicians often make; don't be one of them!

G1062

SET UP THE GROOVE

Let's move up to the next level of playing the bass, playing common bass rhythms and grooves that will enable you to immediately fit in when performing with other musicians.

Before you start, be sure you are very comfortable with the following:
    1) Bass playing technique:
        R.H. techniques (finger alternation, rest strokes, rake, dampening)
        L.H. techniques (shifting, dampening)

    2) Music concepts: basic rhythms, note-reading skills, dynamics, Chord Theory for Bassists Parts 1, 2, and 3, scale theory, be able to easily locate the following on the bass: Roots and Fifths, Primary Chords, any note by name only in at least three places

    3) Music performance: memorize these patterns, Chicago Blues, boogie pattern, ability to play the C and G major scales at a brisk tempo

When you can easily play the music on the following pages, transpose the grooves to other keys.

Let's start off with what we call the "Go-To Rhythm" ♩. ♪ ♩. ♪ which provides more motion than playing straight quarter notes. The Go-To Rhythm works well from slow songs (ballads) to up-tempo tunes. Vary the octaves to create more interest. You can also use this rhythm when learning a new song until you create a more creative groove later.

Video 10

* **Slash Chords:** G is the chord name for guitar or keyboard; B is the note played by the bass.

G1062

Speed Study Boogie

Can you cleanly play this warm-up exercise one time through in 10 seconds? Go!

Playing in 2

The tempo is usually very fast when playing in 2. Many country music songs are played in two.

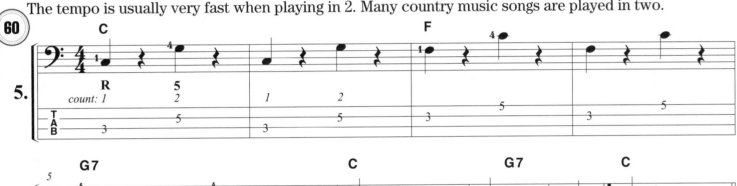

Chicago Blues Variations

Apply these four variations to the Chicago Blues you learned in the Discovery back on page 25.

* Sixteenth and dotted eighth notes: sixteenth notes only get ¼ of one beat, so get to the dotted-eighth note (¾ of one beat) C fast! Listen to the audio often.

Jazz Waltz

62 Review page 21 about using chord names to create a bass line. Here is a walking bass example.

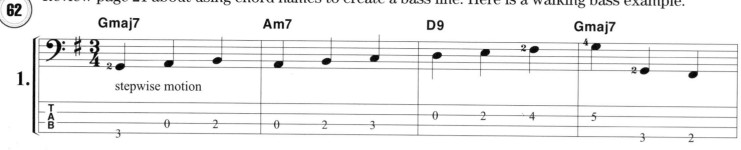

1.

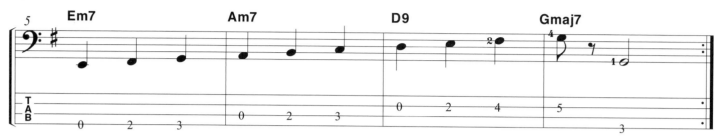

Jazz Waltz Swing

This rhythm is a classic example of a jazz waltz. The musical term **swing** indicates a specific change to the way we play eighth notes. Instead of playing the eighths equally (straight eighths, ½ beat each), in swing style the 1st eighth note in a group of two notes receives ⅔ of a beat and the 2nd eighth note receives only ⅓ of a beat. Think "long   short   long   short."

63

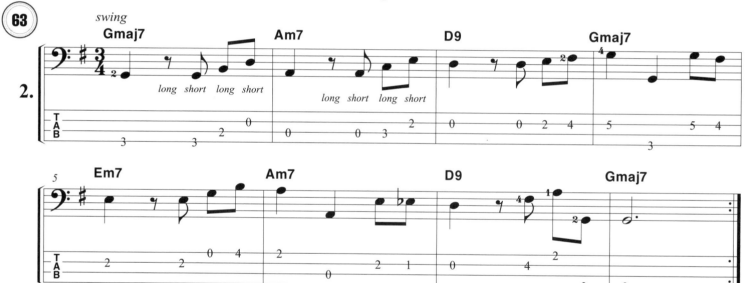

2.

Jazz Walking Bass

Bass players love a walking bass line! The example below shows a **Quick Change**. The IV chord is added in measure two and then back to I in measure three. The Quick Change creates variety with the 12 bar-blues chord changes. Compare these chords to the traditional 12-bar blues on page 43, No. 5.

64

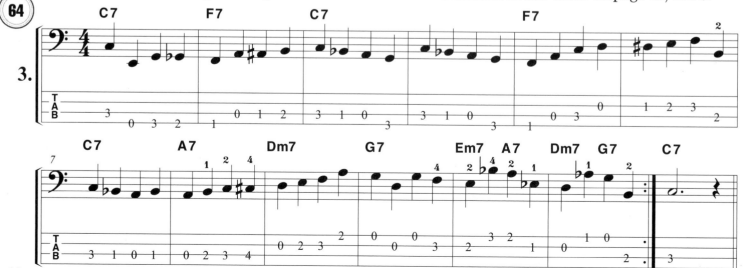

3.

40

The Interval of a 10th

The interval of a 10th is very similar to a third, but with the third one-octave higher. Below you will be playing Am (A - C), Bm (B - D), and Cmaj7 (C - E). Use your right-hand thumb (*t*) and middle finger (*m*). Don't use 10ths too often though, save them for special effects!

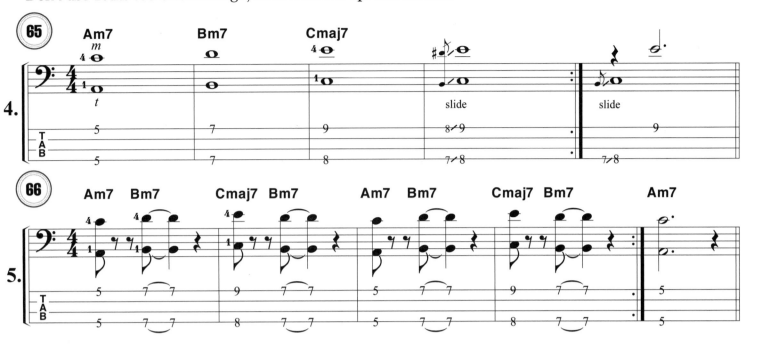

Pedal Point

This is a music technique where a bass note is sustained under a series of chord changes. Using Pedal Point often creates some dissonances but they usually resolve to more pleasant harmonies.

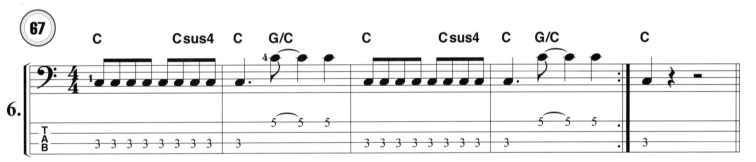

Endings

Many times it is up the bass player to set up the ending for a song. When the band members hear these bass lines they will know that the end is near!

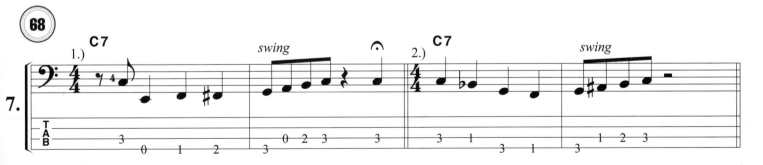

JOB DESCRIPTION, BASS PLAYER

1) Provide a solid bottom that the rest of the band builds upon, like the root of a tree.
2) Play the unchanging groove with a steady beat.
3) Must be able to jump out and play melody when needed.

THE GROOVE

Here we are, this is what playing the bass is all about. Lock in with the drummer (who will eventually become your best friend), and lay down the groove!

Rock Groove 1

The first rock groove is a I (A), vi (F#m), IV (D), V7 (E7) tune. Watch for eighth rests on beat two, be sure there is not any sound coming from your bass.

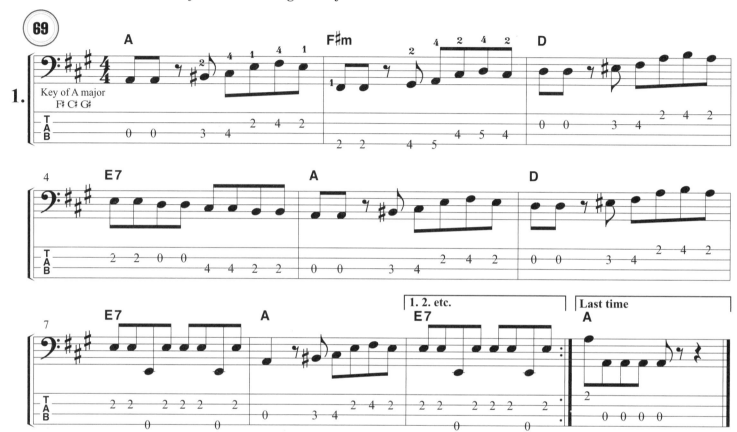

Rock Groove 2

This is a simple yet powerful rock bass line. Play big, don't rush, lay down the groove.

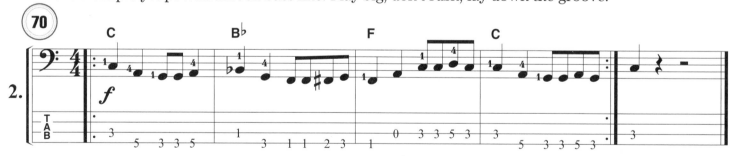

 Famous Music Quotes:

"You can always tell when the groove is working or not." (Prince, 1958-2016)

"When you get a groove going, time flies." (Donald Fagen, 1948-, Steely Dan)

"Life is a lot like jazz … it's best when you improvise!" (George Gershwin, 1898-1937)

"The music is not in the notes, but in the silence between." (Wolfgang Amadeus Mozart, 1756-1791)

"It's not about when the bass does play, it's about when it doesn't play." (Jack Michael Antonoff, 1984-, American musician, singer, songwriter, and record producer)

Motown Groove

In 1960 Berry Gordy, Jr. founded the *Motown Record Company* in Detroit, Michigan. The *Motown Sound* is a popular music style with prominent electric bass lines. Do yourself a favor, *seriously listen* to the bass grooves from these artists: The Funk Brothers (bassist James Jamerson), Marvin Gaye, Smoky Robinson, The Temptations, and many others.

The following Motown Grooves are perfect examples of what the word *groove* means: steady tempo, correct use of rests, and connecting the notes smoothly. When the groove is happening the members of the rhythm section (piano, guitar, bass, and drums) comment, "It ain't nothin' but a thang!"

Funky Blues

A major characteristic of the music scene in the mid 1960s was recording artists merging together the most popular styles of the day. Funk is a combination rhythm and blues (R&B), jazz, and soul music. Rhythm is the main ingredient of funk, meaning that the unusual rhythms of the bass player and the drummmer create a strong, irresistible rhythmic groove, "*so that the dancers just won't hide!*"

When you see the word blues, it will indicate that the chord changes will be primarily be the I, IV, and V chords arranged in the **12 bar-blues** format. Blues tunes generally use seventh chords.

Reggae Groove

To get the best sound, play reggae grooves with your right hand closer to the neck.

Reggae grooves use a lot of 16th notes (♪♪♪♪) and 16th rests (𝄾). There is no need to get too technical yet, so for now, just be aware that 16th notes are faster than 8th notes. Four 16th notes beamed together (with two beams) equal 1 beat. Listen to the audio tracks often!

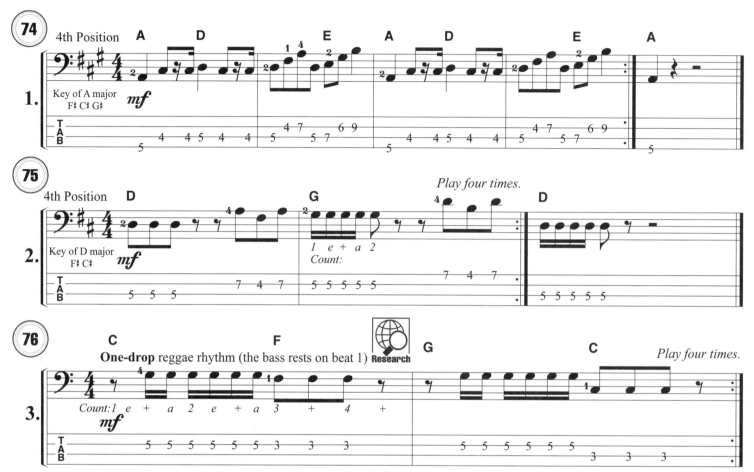

Boogie Groove

You will be using the boogie bass pattern often in your playing career. There are many variations of the boogie, create your own! The pattern below can be moved around to *any* position because there are no open strings.

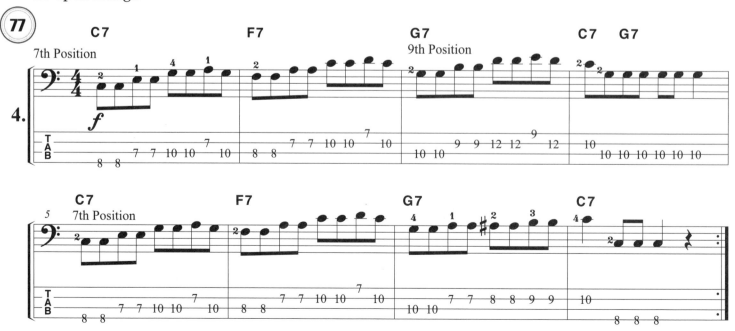

Jazz Grooves

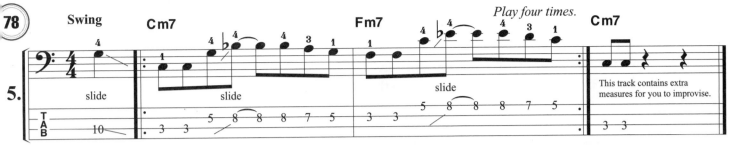

 Rhythm Changes is a term referring to the chord progression from a famous George Gershwin tune entitled, *I Got Rhythm*. These chord changes are well suited for improvisation, which explains why there are many jazz compositions that follow this exact chord progression. The music below is a melody for electric bass using only the first sixteen measures of the *Rhythm Changes*. Track 81 contains four additional versions of this chord progression using bass grooves you have already learned. Listen to this track often, *I Got Rhythm* is a jazz classic!

G1062

ADVANCED TECHNIQUE

Music "technique" refers to the ability of musicians to demonstrate they have confidence and control of their instruments so that they can play with ease and great precision. The classical guys work on technique; rock/pop performers have "chops", as in saying, "That bass player has some chops!" Let's get to work on your chops!

There are many techniques books and videos on the market. They almost all start playing **scales**, which can be easily memorized and played with a metronome to build up stamina and speed, but above all accuracy. Start at about ♩ = 60 on your metronome and then gradually increase the tempo. A good practice tip is to play the appropriate scale before playing a song.

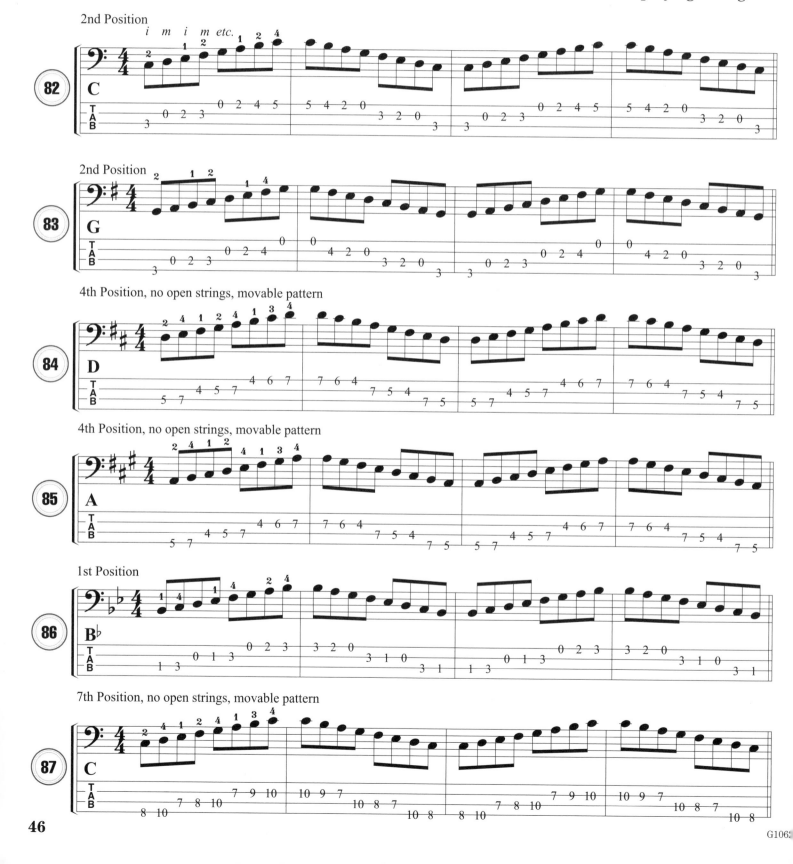

G106

NEED TO KNOW

Developing musicians "develop" by hearing and studying other musicians whom they admire. Likewise there are many recorded examples that define the perimeters of their instrument. Below are two lists that you "need to know!"

There is one thing for sure about our favorite songs in popular music, all of them owe a significant chunk of their awesomeness to their bass lines.

We have put together a list of bass players (in our opinion) that made this happen. These artists helped us to be the performers we are today. Maybe you will want to add several of these extraordinary bassists to your list! Pick three performers that you identify with and do extended research on them.

Bassists Name - Genre (Performing Group or Albums)

Bootsy Collins - Funk (James Brown, Parliment-Funkadelic)

Cachao (Israel López Valdés) - Latin, double bass (the most influential bass player of Cuban music)

Carol Kaye - Pop, Rock (The Wrecking Crew, hundreds of hit records in the 60s and 70s)

Charlie Mingus - Jazz, double bass (bassist with Miles Davis, Duke Ellington, Charlie Parker, many others)

Donald (Duck) Dunn - R&B, Soul, Blues (Booker T. and the M.G.'s, Stax Records, The Blues Brothers)

Esperanza Spalding - Jazz, electric and double bass (Recording Artist with five albums)

Flea (Michael Balzary) - Rock (Red Hot Chili Peppers)

Getty Lee - Rock, Progressive Rock (Rush)

Jack Bruce - Rock (Cream)

Larry Graham - Rock, slap bass (Sly and the Family Stone)

Linda Oh - Jazz, electric and double bass (Recording Artist with four albums, toured with Pat Metheny)

Jaco Pastorius - Jazz, fretless bass (Weather Report, Solo Career)

James Jamerson - R&B, Soul (Motown, The Funk Brothers)

Paul McCartney - Pop, Rock (The Beatles, Wings, Solo Career)

Rocco Prestia - Rock, Funk (Tower of Power)

Stanley Clark - Jazz, Electric and double bass (Return to Forever, Solo Career)

Tal Wilkenfield - Rock, Jazz, electric bass (Recording Artist with two albums, toured with Jeff Beck)

Victor Wooten - Pop, Rock (Béla Fleck and the Flecktones, SMV)

Here is our list of riffs and tunes that you need to know! Listen to all of these tunes and then add other tunes that you enjoy playing to this list. Make it a point to learn the basic riffs of at least three of these great songs!

Tune - Artist

All My Loving - The Beatles

Another One Bites the Dust - Pink Floyd

Brick House - The Commodores

Chameleon - Herbie Hancock

Come On, Come Over - Jaco Pastorius

Come Together - The Beatles

Disco Inferno - The Trammps

I Heard It Through the Grapevine - Gladys Knight

I Saw Her Standing There - The Beatles

I'll Take You There - Staple Singers

Money - Pink Floyd

My Generation - The Who

My Girl - The Temptations

Seven Nation Army - The White Stripes

She Caught the Katy - The Blues Brothers

Soul Man - Sam and Dave

Stand by Me - Ben E. King

Sunshine of Your Love - Cream

What is Hip? - Tower of Power

GLOSSARY

SIGN	TERM	DEFINITION
	accidentals	sharps (♯), flats (♭), and naturals (♮) (pg. 28)
	dampening	Using the left or right hand to stop the strings from sounding. (pg. 27)
𝄐	**fermata**	Indicates that a note or a rest should be held longer than usual. (pg. 27)
	harmony	Musical pitches played at the same time; chords. (pg. 10)
	major scale	A series of pitches arranged stepwise in ascending and descending order. (pg. 3?)
	melody	The notes to a song; how the song goes. (pg. 26)
	N.C.	No chords are to be played. (pg. 24)
	octave	Notes with the same name that are eight steps apart. (pg. 31)
	pick-up notes	One or more notes that are played before the first complete measure of music. (pg. 13)
	pitch	the highness of lowness of a note (pg. 11)
	position	Assigning left-hand fingers to certain frets. (pg. 8)
𝄇	**repeat sign**	Play a section of music again after seeing this sign. (pg. 14)
𝄽	**rests**	Indicate a moment of silence in music. (pg. 27)
	rhythm	The timing of the music using different note values. (pg. 4)
	sixteenth notes	A sixteenth note receive ¼ of one beat. Four sixteenths equal 1 beat. (pg. 39)
G/B	**slash chord**	A chord in which the lowest-pitched note is not the root. G/B is a G chord with a B in the bass. As a bassist, you will play the B. (pg. 38)
	slide	A technique where a left-hand finger slides from one note to another. (pg. 41)
	steps	Notes that are one letter name apart, moving in *line-space* or *space-line* order. A half step is the distance of one fret. A whole step is the distance of two frets. (pg. 32)
	swing	Playing eighth notes in a long-short rhythm rather than ½ beat each. (pg. 40)
	unison	Two notes with the exact pitch. (pg. 29)

G106